I FOUND A BABY RABBIT, WHAT DO I DO?

DALE CARLSON
ILLUSTRATED BY HOPE M. DOUGLAS

WIND OVER WINGS PRESS
BICK PUBLISHING HOUSE

Text © copyright 1994 by Dale Carlson
      © illustrations 1994 by Hope M. Douglas
Second Edition, 1995

Edited by Ann Maurer
Book design by Jane Miller
Cover design by Stan Park

With thanks to our veterinarian, Richard A. Alter D.V.M.

WIND OVER WINGS PRESS is a trademark of
BICK PUBLISHING HOUSE

ISBN: 1-884158-03-x -- Volume 4
ISBN: 1-884158-04-8 -- 6 Volume Set

Printed by Royal Printing Service, Guilford, Connecticut, USA

Note

Even though helping hurt and distressed animals seems like an easy thing to do, it isn't always as simple as it looks.

It may require a legal permit in your state to raise and release wildlife.

Call your Department of Environmental Protection for advice, for the telephone number of your nearest local rehabilitator, for information on how you can get training and your own permit.

Contents

Acknowledgements

Our gratitude to the network of Wind Over Wings rehabilitators and its associated rehabilitator friends: Irene Ruth, founder and director of Suburban Wildlife; Cathy Zamecnik; Dawn and Job Day, Susanne Colten-Carey; Hope Douglas, founder and director of Wind Over Wings, and Tamara Miglio its president and our copy editor.

Our special thanks to Dan Mackey, publisher of Wildlife Rehabilitation Today Magazine, and to International Wildlife Rehabilitation Council for their inspiration and high standards of excellence.

And our thanks to Herb Swartz for his kindness and his computers.

I FOUND A BABY RABBIT, WHAT DO I DO?

WHY SAVE A BABY RABBIT AT ALL?

After all, there are so many rabbits.

A boy watched a rehabilitator nurture and feed, raise and release, baby rabbit after baby rabbit after baby rabbit all spring and all summer long. Orphaned and injured young rabbits were found and brought to the rehabilitator who thought nothing of night-long vigils or driving many miles to the veterinarian. The care was constant. So were the numbers of incoming and outgoing bunnies.

The boy marveled at a long, exhausting night of surgery over one tiny cottontail and said, "But there are so many of them. Why does this baby rabbit matter so much?"

And the rehabilitator answered, "It matters to the baby rabbit."

Rehabilitators are dedicated to saving lives, not to deciding what forms of life are worth saving.

Rehabilitators take no hostages for their own sake, but release for the sake of the animal. Rabbits rarely live more than a year in the wild and as much as seven years in captivity, but free is free.

Rehabilitators, surrogate parents, teach all it is possible to teach and reward with freedom, not the captivity of barred cages.

REHABILITATORS UNDERSTAND THE LIMITS OF REHABILITATION: ANY SICK OR INJURED ADULT, OR INFANT OR JUVENILE, NEEDS TO BE TAKEN TO A VETERINARIAN UNLESS YOU HAVE THE NECESSARY SKILLS.

WHY RABBITS GET HURT

Most rabbits nest on the ground. They get hurt from: people trampling over their nests; the cats and dogs that belong to people attacking them; the people driving lawnmowers into their homes. They are hunted by people with guns and killed with people's pesticides. They are too quick, mostly, for roadkill by cars.

Nature helps. Raccoons prey on rabbits. So do hawks, owls, ferrets, and any assortment of larger predators. Storms wreck their nests. Too much rain drowns. Too little parches.

But whether it is us or nature who hurts them, they need our help.

WAIT   WATCH   WARM

If you find a nest of babies, watch if first for an hour or so.

To rehabilitate well, it is important to understand wildlife in the wild. Rabbits are wilder than most, and must be understood in the wild to help them properly.

Before the birth of a litter, the mother prepares a nest in the earth, usually lining it with grass and fur plucked from her own abdomen. The doe often stays away from her babies in the nest, so as not to draw the attention of predators. She watches them from some distance. AN ABSENT MOTHER IS NORMAL – DO NOT BUNNYNAP UNTIL YOU ARE SURE THE BABIES ARE ORPHANED. Remember, too, that rabbits are nocturnal and feed from dusk to dawn, so she will often be away even at night.

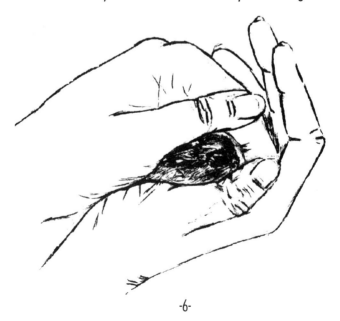

But she will return on and off all night. At dusk, take two sticks and cross them in an X over the nest. If they are disturbed in the morning, the mother has returned, if undisturbed, the babies are orphans. The mother has been killed.

If a pet brings you a single baby — baby rabbits do not often wander from the nest on their own — first try to find the nest.

IMPORTANT NOTE: Young rabbits who are able to be on their own are small. Do not try to capture any rabbit the size of your fist or larger. Any attempt to round one up will likely give it a heart attack from shock and it will die. If you have to chase it, it probably doesn't need to be rescued!

Once you are sure your small rabbit is motherless and too little to be on its own, CARE BEGINS.

Warm the baby. Make a nest of your hands. Be very careful to keep the baby covered as babies rabbits are like coiled springs and will squirt out of your hands if they are startled. Unlike other mammals, baby rabbits should not be cuddled because they go into shock so easily. Handle them as little as possible.

A sad warning: orphaned and injured rabbits are difficult to raise and release and their death rate in captivity is high.

Don't be frightened. A baby rabbit doesn't bite.

If you find a nest of babies, scoop up some of the bedding of grass and fur and carry it with the babies in your hands. Or go and bring a small box with a cover. Line the box with paper toweling or a soft, unstringy cloth and some of the original bedding material for familiarity. For the sake of cleanliness, you will discard this after twenty-four hours. Be sure the box has breathing holes. Be sure to cover the box and tape it securely. Even young baby rabbits jump!

You will need the help of a licensed rehabilitator to care for the baby. This is true even if you are a practiced rehabilitator of other species but without experience with rabbits. This is true even more if the rabbit is injured or has symptoms of severe dehydration or disease.

DO keep it warm. **DO NOT** feed it food or water right away.

Place your rabbit, or rabbits, in a warm, quiet, semi-dark place. You will need two boxes: a small box for a nest, and a large one to put the nest inside of.

Make the nest box out of a small wooden or cardboard box, with the opening at one side. Line this with a soft cloth. Or you can simulate the original nest by using two washcloths: one folded up with a depression in it and the other laid over the top. It is important for the rabbit baby to have a private place to be in.

At first, a cardboard box will do for the larger container. An aquarium with a wire mesh cover is fine. Line it with paper toweling, or an old T-shirt or clean flannel cloth or piece of sheet. Never colored newspaper (poison), and no shredding towels (to catch nails or choke in). It is important besides to use white material so you can see when the babies begin to urinate on their own.

It is particularly important to keep your dog and cat away from the baby rabbit. It particularly important to make certain the rabbit can't jump out of whatever housing it is in.

Put the baby inside the nest, and the nest inside the large container. Later, when the eyes are open, you can add leaves and clover and grass for your rabbit to use as nesting material, small leafy limbs for cover, bark, twigs, whatever its original natural environment suggests.

As the rabbits become larger, the size and depth of the box must be adjusted. Rabbits can jump unbelievably high at an early age, and because they hate captivity, will jump at the sides of whatever box or cage you keep them in. Hang cloth — cut up bedding pads are excellent — on the sides of the housing.

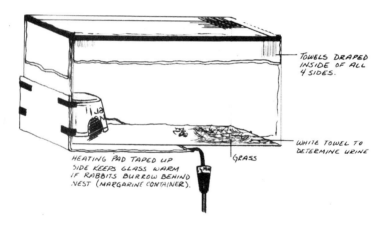

TOWELS DRAPED INSIDE OF ALL 4 SIDES.

WHITE TOWEL TO DETERMINE URINE

HEATING PAD TAPED UP SIDE KEEPS GLASS WARM IF RABBITS BURROW BEHIND NEST (MARGARINE CONTAINER).

GRASS

Now, continue to keep your baby warm. KEEP IT WARM BUT NEVER HOT! A heating pad turned low under the nest and up the side of the outer box will be fine. Keep all heating appliances outside the outer box. Inside, it should feel warm to the touch, cosy, not hot.

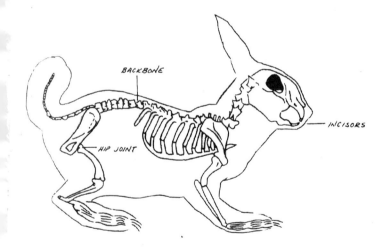

BACKBONE

INCISORS

HIP JOINT

YOUR RABBIT IS HUNGRY

DO NOT feed it yet. If there is dehydration, give rehydration fluid orally. Severe rehydration requires a vet's subcutaneous injection. When your bunny is warm, use a small plastic dropper, syringe with or without the nipple, or a pet nurser, to give the following special drink called a rehydrating solution. (Never do this with a cold animal.)

A PROPER HOLDING TECHNIQUE.

Squeeze a drop or two at a time into the bunny's mouth. Wait until it is swallowed. Go slowly and gently to prevent aspiration, or inhalation pneumonia. This is when the baby sucks the fluid in up its nose and into its lungs.

1 teaspoon salt		1/3 teaspoon salt
3 Tablespoons sugar	OR	1 Tablespoon sugar
1 quart warm water		1 cup warm water

The above is a homemade solution. Commercially available electrolyte solutions such as Pedialyte (any baby formula section of the supermarket) can also be given.

Offer 1cc or 2cc's every two hours.

Let your rabbit rest quietly in between rehydration feedings.

Quiet is the most important word for captive rabbits. They have been known to bruise their eyes, hurt their backs, hit their heads and break their necks on the top of their housing in a panic stampede.

Find out what kind of rabbit you have

EASTERN COTTONTAIL
14 9/16 - 18 1/4"

EUROPEAN RABBIT
18 - 24"

MARSH RABBIT
14 1/8 - 18"

CAPE HARE
25 1/4 - 27 3/4"

FIND OUT WHAT KIND OF RABBIT YOU HAVE

Look at your rabbit again carefully. Then look at a really good wildlife mammal book. You will find a good book at your public library if you don't own one.

Here is a page of some common rabbits

1. Cottontails: Eastern, Mountain, Desert, New England

2. Brush rabbit, Pygmy rabbit, Swamp rabbit, Marsh rabbit

3. Blacktail jackrabbit, European hare

BLACK-TAILED
JACK RABBIT
18¼ -24¾"

You need to find out your rabbit's age to feed it the proper diet and house it in the proper way.

Here is a page of rabbits at different ages and stages of development.

Infant: naked, eyes closed, ears flat, 3-4 inches long

Juvenile: a week to ten days, fully furred, eyes open; two to three weeks investigating greens, soft solids, sometimes lapping formula

Sub-adult: three to four weeks, weaned from bottle, eating greens and solids, ready for release even if the white spot has not disappeared, 4-5 inches long, very afraid of humans

Do not keep bunnies in captivity longer than 5-6 weeks. Different aged bunnies eat differently. The wrong food fed wrongly will not help your bunny to grow properly.

NEWBORN COTTONTAIL
3-4" LONG, EYES CLOSED

JUVENILE

ADULT

Your baby rabbit check list.

1. You have got your bunny warm, rested, and calm.

2. You have seen it is not too hurt or stressed.

3. You have given it rehydration fluid.

4. You have identified your baby rabbit and its age in your book and probably read as well about its natural habitat, natural foods, natural habits. All of this will help you care for it better.

FEEDING YOUR BABY RABBIT

You begin by mixing formula, just as you would for any baby mammal. The baby rabbit's formula is a little different from that used for infant squirrels, raccoons, woodchucks, because its intestinal environment is different. There are disagreements about formula components and how often to feed baby rabbits.

This is what we are doing currently.

Mix:

3 parts boiled water

1 part Esbilac powder

2 parts heavy whipping cream

Bactrim® .02 ml 2x per day for first week to reduce bacteria, to prevent diarrhea

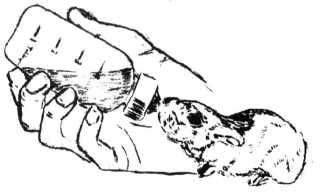

When starting formula, do it gradually.

3/4 parts rehydration solution, 1/4 part formula
1/2 part rehydration solution, 1/2 part formula
1/4 part rehydration solution, 3/4 part formula

For infant bunnies whose eyes are still closed, a plastic dropper or syringe with nipple may work better than a pet nurser. You can control the flow better – never more in the mouth than is being swallowed to prevent aspiration.

You will hear controversy among rehabilitators about how often to feed. We feed every six hours three times per day from 7 a.m. to 11 p.m. when the bunnies' eyes are closed. Pink hairless bunnies eat 1/2 cc of warm formula every three hours 6x per day. Bunnies with closed eyes and flat ears will eat about 2cc per feeding. Increase amounts as the bunny grows from 2cc's to 5cc's per feeding. Start to wean from the bottle at three weeks, by eliminating one feeding at a time, the middle one first. They should be weaned by the time they are three to four weeks old.

IMPORTANT. For the first week, stimulate your bunny's genital area after feeding so it can urinate. Unless stimulated, a bunny may die. Stimulate with a damp tissue or cotton ball or Q-tip. They may leave their pepper-like droppings on their own, but wait until you see signs of urination on their cage flooring before stopping the stimulation.

To avoid stress during this procedure, stimulate only for a minute and stop, whether they urinate or not.

IMPORTANT. Never overfeed. A bunny's tummy should be full and round — not tight. Like a marshmellow. Introduce solid foods when the eyes are open. Offer rolled oats, commercial rabbit pellets, fresh greens like clover, dandelion greens, wild carrot greens, alfalfa hay, twigs and bark to chew, fruit tree leaves and blossoms— they love wisteria leaves and blossoms— leafy lettuce, apple bits, sunflower seeds, corn, carrots. Rabbits need balanced diets that include grain, fruit, balanced rabbit feed.

Add a small jar cap of water to the cage during and after weaning. If they do not seem to drink, sprinkle the veggies and fruits with water. A pan of dirt for dust baths has been suggested in some manuals. And keep leafy branches and grasses about to provide cover for your rabbits as they will frighten more and more easily.

Remember: at 3-5 weeks, your rabbit should be off formula, onto solids, and ready for release. RABBITS HATE CAPTIVITY.

MAKE A PROPER HOME FOR YOUR RABBITS

You have already made a small nest burrow, a box with tissues, or small, clean cloth inside it, and placed it inside a larger container, aquarium with wire-mesh cover, hardware-clothed dog crate, or a wire carrying cage. This is excellent for the first two weeks. Do clean the tissues whenever dirty, as unsanitary conditions can quickly cause serious, often fatal, diseases.

As the rabbits grow and open their eyes at about two weeks of age, caging must be enlarged, to give more room for movement and more space for food, and to help alleviate stress. Two eyes-open bunnies may be caged in an 18" pet carrying cage; three or four (litter is 4-5) in a 2'x 3' and 18" high cage.

Wire cages could be made of 1/2" hardware cloth. Cage bottoms must be flush to prevent leg injuries, or put newspaper on floor grid. And, as previously mentioned, hang soft, padded cloth to sides and top to prevent banging injury when bunnies leap from sudden fright. Cover bottom of cages with not-shredding or paper toweling or sheeting over newspaper. Remember, lots of hiding places and cover. Leafy branches are good. Or piles of grass.

Try not to mix bunny groups. Fighting may occur. It is always better to bring up baby rabbits with one or more of their own kind, however, so if you do mix two or three from different groups, watch them carefully for the first twenty-four hours.

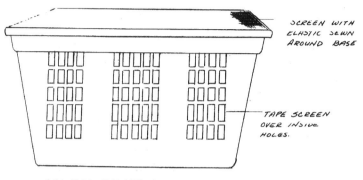

SCREEN WITH
ELASTIC SEWN
AROUND BASE

TAPE SCREEN
OVER INSIDE
HOLES.

LAUNDRY BASKET HOME.
NEST BOX INSIDE, BRANCHES.
GREENS

WIRE MESH

PRE-RELEASE HOME : WIRE CRATE
COVERED WITH HARDWARE CLOTH

RELEASING YOUR RABBITS

DO NOT keep healthy rabbits after five weeks.

At five weeks old or so, your rabbits are ready for release. They are not full grown, but they are able to care for themselves and do not do well in captivity now. You are no longer handling them. For one thing, they squirt from your hands. For another it scares them, sometimes literally, to death.

They are self-feeding.

You have not habituated (gotten them used to) any household pets or yourself.

They have been conditioned to outside temperatures by leaving their cage outside during the day for three days.

They are going crazy in their cage, anyway.

It is time for letting go.

Your rabbits were born free.

You have taught them all they need to live free, especially about food and enemies.

Make sure the weather forecast is good for at least three days.

Release in the early evening, or early morning.

Leave rabbit pellets at release site, although rabbits probably will not come back as squirrels and raccoons do.

Release in a location where there are plenty of grazing areas plus wooded areas for shelter. Release away from humans, dogs, and cats.

It is up to you to decide on the best environment for them.

But if baby rabbits are alive, you have done a successful rehabilitation and release.

The release is the most important after the saving part of rehabilitation. Wildlife is not ours to keep, but to help in its distress and let go.

You have done this.

RELEASE. LAUNDRY BASKET USED TO CARRY
RABBIT TO RELEASE SITE. SCREEN TOP.

You miss your rabbits.
What can you do?

Your rabbit may grow strong and when released hop right out of your life and into a life of its own.

Or it may not thrive and grow strong. Sometimes a rabbit hurts too much and dies. It is not your fault. You did your best. You protected its living and dying, kept it fed, warmed, and safe from predators.

You cared.
Growing away is part of rehabilitating.
Dying is part of rehabilitating.
Both ways, your rabbit has gone.
What can you do?
You know.
Help another one.

HOT TIPS FOR YOU

1. Don't handle a rabbit if you don't want to.

2. Call for help and advice.

3. Don't animalnap a baby rabbit. Watch for mother before rescuing. Never rescue a rabbit the size of your fist or larger, unless it is injured. You can shock it into a heart attack.

4. Your goal in rescuing a rabbit is its release when possible. No critter wants a life prison sentence unless it's too hurt to survive. Especially rabbits can get suicidal in captivity.

5. If you find an injured adult rabbit, wear gloves.

6. Keep any critter away from your face.

7. Wash hands first for rabbit's sake.

8. Wash hands after handling for your own sake.

HOT TIPS FOR CRITTERS

1. In the case of found babies, watch for mother first: DON'T CRITTERNAP while mother is watching from a distance or off finding food.

2. Warm rabbit first in your hands, or against your body.

3. Put in warm, quiet, dark place to recover from shock. In rabbit's case, handle always as little as possible.

4. Generally, it's a good idea to give rehydration solution before food.

5. NEVER FEED a cold, starving critter before warming and rehydrating.

6. Keep household pets away however gentle. Rabbits and other small wildlife need to learn to fear cats and dogs.

7. Call Department of Environmental Protection, or your local wildlife rehabilitator, for advice and help. Your vet or local police will have telephone numbers.

Reference books:

PETERSON FIELD GUIDE SERIES, A Field Guide to the Mammals of North America north of Mexico, A Field Guide to Birds (regional), by Roger Tory Peterson, Houghton, Mifflin Company, Boston.

STOKES NATURE GUIDES, A Guide to Animal Tracking and Behavior, A Guide to Bird Behavior, Volume I,II,III, by Donald Stokes, Little, Brown and Company, Boston

AUDUBON HANDBOOKS, Mcgraw-Hill Book Company, New York, San Francisco, Singapore, Toronto, et al.

Recommended manuals:

WILDLIFE RESCUE, INC., Austin, Texas.

WILDLIFE CARE AND REHABILITATION, Brukner Nature Center, Troy, Ohio.

WILD ANIMAL CARE AND REHABILITATION, The Kalamazoo Nature Center, Kalamazoo, Michigan.

BASIC WILDLIFE REHABILITATION, 1AB, International Wildlife Rehabilitation Council, Suisun, California.

INTRODUCTION TO WILDLIFE REHABILITATION, National Wildlife Rehabilitators Association, Carpenter Nature Center, Hastings, Minnesota.

Notes

Notes